SAY YES

Other books by j.d.

Nonfiction

The Old Wolf Lady: A Biography

Poetry

Currents that Puncture: A Dissertation

Say Yes

j.d. daniels

Savvy Press

New York

Say Yes

Copyright@ 2013 by j.d. daniels

Cover Art by Peg Cullen & Andi McCarter

All rights reserved. No part of this book may be used or reproduced in any manner whatsoever without written permission except in the case of brief quotations embodied in critical articles or reviews. For information address Savvy Press, http://www.savvypress.com/

This is a work of the imagination. Names, characters, places, and incidents are either the product of the author's creative mind or are used factiously, and any resemblance to actual persons, living or dead, business establishments, events or locales is entirely coincidental.

ISBN: 978-1-939113-13-9

Library of Congress Control Number: 2013908356

Printed in the United States of America

Savvy Press 2013

…we all begin the process before we are ready, before we are strong enough, before we know enough…

> ~ Clarissa Pinkola Estes, Women Who Run With the Wolves: Myths and Stories of the Wild Women Archetypes

For

those who

jumped

or may jump into the fire

Inside you there's an artist you don't know about… say yes quickly, if you know, if you've known it from before the beginning of the universe

~ Rumi, thirteenth century Sufi teacher, mystic and poet

CONTENTS

Wraps	1
A Message for Hemingway	2
Tides in Retrospect	5
Corea, Maine Shadows	9
The Gallery Visit	11
Three Females in Art	13
Framed in Silence	15
Diabolical Hands	17
Nancy's Woodcut	20
Drawing in Charcoal	23
After Seeing "Waiting on the Moon"	25
Breakfast at McDonald's	26
Snow Bombs	28
March Graveside Visit	30
Ghazal of the Now	33
The Crossroads	35

Maneuvering the Big Dipper	37
The Green Theatre	39
That Night	42
The Fish Hook	46
The Park Pond	48
Blinking Neon	50
The Intrusion	52
A Sunday After	55
Clinging Snow	57
Sacred Anasashi World	59
The Riderless Horse	61
The Third Tier	62
In Maria's Waking Dream	64
The Disappearing String	66
Days Gone By	67
Mount Ayr	69
Laying Sod	70
Blow it Up	72

White Wolf at Her Side	73
Balloon Days	74
There Is More Light	76
Pelican Totem	78
Blessed with Choice	79
Ole House	80
The Pelican	82
Say Yes	83
Acknowledgments	85
About the Poet and Author	87

Wraps

And you? When will you begin that long journey into yourself? ~ Rumi

She sits alone wrapped in her green coat

like an eagle writhing to burst her shell

fearful as she gazes into her cup

half-hidden by the shadows of the night

The woman   like the artist

is aware of the darkness behind her

He has painted the picture window ominous

making her figure small before it

She poses knowing his purpose

but unwilling to turn to the void

Though the blackened window reflects a pathway of light

the woman waits   yet unable to shed her wrap

A Message for Hemingway

When you do things from your soul, you feel a

river moving in you, a joy ~ Rumi

I painted your house once you know

standing on your sidewalk

looking at the plantains

the hibiscus in pale bloom

smelling the lushness

mixed with the salt air

capturing your spooled steps

in shades of grey

You didn't see me   of course

How could you? You weren't there

but then   neither was I

Painting your house   the one

with the tiered front porch

as the aged wicker rocker

whispered in the breeze

I stroked the canvas

thinking of Brett   of her failed dreams

Catching the scrubs with touches

of ochre and cadmium red

But the windows   I could never

get the windows

They became lost within

the viridian shutters

Now that painting hangs not at my home

but over my mother's quilt-covered bed

Hanging between the dark wooden

fork and spoon from Mexico

near the gold and black tapestry

brought from Greece

the one with the stag eating

secure in its place miles from the Keys

at home amongst the fields of corn

with an existence all its own

Tides in Retrospect

The lion is most handsome when looking for food

~ Rumi

On that bouldered coast where tides

inhale and exhale like a vomiting child

dropping its bowels among chiseled copper crevices

We leaped the crags as gulls swooped for eel

feeling the pall of earth breathing our depths of

immaturity while our children explored the sea with its

seizures amid grays   blues   corals   and shadows

Years before we lived southward where seas flowed

like one-hundred pound tortoises hauled in from waters

We   devouring one-clawed lobsters netted

in currents that puncture

As the salt-filled ceiling filtered on our caresses

we laughed at the acts impropriety

while that forgotten other slept in silence

like a displaced northern teal

On days when Pelicans swarmed the fishing boat's keel

I felt the heat of hook plunge within tallow

as you pulled in Jewfish   Mackerel   and   Wahoo

The thirty-five millimeter flashed wild

while the captain maneuvered to shore touched

by snowbirds in reverence

as though he were an esthetic Jaine

sweeping his path in composure

The handprint factory smelled

of perfumed oils in tincture

The Conch train a limpid sea otter

bearing tourists like Erendira's entourage

in vicarious vices

with the tattooed white whale in comfort on pillows

Brown boys peddling their shells   hiding their bile

Regge beating its Jamaican rhythm

while flesh burnt to purity

We saw Hemingway's stilt-house set in quiet simplicity

rotting through ages by exposure

Surrounded by the sea sitting languid   unriled

Spending our days showing sights like

an old-fashioned newsreel

as if we were the church elders and they the hallowed

I   taking my place behind the pews   waiting

for my cue at the service

Starred nights we walked the beach viewing blemishes

Smelling the rankness of the tide's droppings

My wish now to recall those times of mellow

To envision the young girl who stood delayed

as in a stilled-shot feature

Not fervent to escape the bonds of youth that sealed

the film in its gray canister marked   Dead Filed

As insipid seas flow   I now stand among

chiseled copper crevices

inhaling the currents that puncture   No longer a

northern teal   nor sitting languid   unriled

but pushing for flesh burnt to purity

Corea, Maine Shadows

A voice inside the beat says, "I know you're tired,

but come. This is the way ~ Rumi

Remember that shingled cottage grayed with salt

where the flag swayed in early light

and the aged Ben Franklin

simmered with the coals of driftwood?

We   filling the twin pine

rockers   unaware of their untold tales

as the Atlantic roared its pleasure

conquering the mountainous boulders in triumph

like a Dali figure balancing the sea on his knee

The journey to Frankenstein's department store

maneuvered that day bringing bewilderment

as we viewed the tiny five and ten

The shopping center promised   denied

like Madeline's vision come alive

on St. Agnes Eve

Silencing

as Angela's antique face

Memories forgotten in the darkness

of the attic

                without forgiveness

The Gallery Visit

Raise your words, not voice.

It is rain that grows flowers,

not thunder ~ Rumi

We don't allow no sketching he said

That's OK   I'm going to write a poem

I laughed

How funny that he should think I could draw

Me   walking these white walled halls

searching for inspiration

only to find ropes hung

I sit across from a photograph

of disjointed female torsos

Mannequins used as symbols

to show the human condition

A head divided symmetrically with masking tape

one leg bent at the knee

Another Renaissance mask

lies near an outstretched foot

No unity in this black and white image

Cross-legged   I relax on the oak hardwood floor

directing my gaze from the photo entitled "Mothers"

that hangs near by

Two stark faces

with sand at their feet

and storm clouds in the sky

While the man in the navy blue blazer

paces by nervously checking my progress

Three Females in Art

Each has to enter the nest made by the other

imperfect bird ~ Rumi

I often wonder what the curator thinks

when placing the paintings

on the gallery walls

This day I sit in front of "Nicole and her Mother"

red cheeks pensive

eyes downcast

The mother's Stygian hair in a high bun upon her head

This painting hangs beside the

Tahitian Gauguin

she   too   a mother?

Yet   her hands push away

the unforeseen

Two paintings of women

side by side

The red frame repelling

the gold filigree

with the Polynesian floating arm

bent slightly at the elbow

in the background

holding

nothing

behind the naked

woman in crimson

Framed in Silence

Move outside the tangle of fear-thinking.

Live in silence ~ Rumi

Mummified figures

climb multi-directional stairs

Shadows of Coleridge's opium dream

in this piece of art

entitled "Relativity"

One couple sits eating

Another faceless twosome stroll

arms intertwined

their wrapped feet inches from the ground

like Dali's wife Gala

suspended above her chair

My eyes fix upon

one lone figure

who stands

two steps from the top

held in abeyance

unable to continue

Head down

Shoulders curled

Outstretched fingers

digging into her father's

flannel shirt

Mutations

framed in silence

within this surreal world

of the artist

Diabolical Hands

It is God's loving kindness to terrify you,

in order to lead you to

His Kingdom of safety ~ Rumi

There they are

the shadowed children

dancing

within the uncouth grove of trees

Not a vision at all

but reality

while diabolical hands

force a child

onto a boulder

and the encircling dancers

beat their soles

in discordant rhythm

The blindfolded streetwalker is led

by the muscular boar on a lease

A magnificent gold and blue bow hangs

under the lady's painted breasts

Black stockings reach for her thighs

as silver heels trimmed in pale pink shimmer

and angels fly above her head

She   seemingly   content to be led

I   wondering what Crane's Maggie

would have aspired to

if she had had such guidance

My mind wanders

to a time of primordial purity

when flesh stretched skyward

and women trekked to the hand-dug

wells for their water

among impersonal mountains

Those women too attuned to the angelic face

of the visionary

who hovered silent

with the lamb and dog at his feet?

The daydreamer sits in a tree

a white morning glory

droops from her tanned fingers

well hidden among the thickness

of the pygmy leaves

unwilling to expose herself

Unlike the red-eyed Thracian girl

moaning at the severed head of Orpheus

when March plantings sprouted

out of hollow-eyed girls

and women's necks were imprisoned

in emeralds   diamonds   and   gold

Nancy's Woodcut

Why do you stay in prison when the door

is so wide open? ~ Rumi

Nancy's face penetrates the paintings

Solemn   one eye curiously

larger   Dine's only female subject

etched in blacks   grays   pale

rose   always with that single

eye seeming to perceive more

She must have sat for him for hours

In Paris   in the Holy Land   at 12 Rue Jacob

Then I stood before the woodcut

What did she think when she saw it

to be forever framed?

The artist applying his final touches

using his electric tool

working painstakingly

to show the world his genius

Drilling while she brewed his tea   made his bed

Calling her in as he stood back in triumph

Nancy   come see   It's finished

She   wiping the soap from her

hands   snipping the dead

leaves from the geraniums on the

sill   carrying the dishcloth with her

How she must have stood and viewed her

image in the five foot expanse of

wood   How he had captured her fine cheek

bones   chiseled her long nose

the eye staring

back   silently taking in his

art   Her vision entering her

slowly   Stepping one foot

closer   the towel careening to the

floor as she saw how

carefully he had done his

work   How the throat had been carved

away   the voice box now

missing   the wood chips scattered

on the floor

Stooping   she swept each tiny particle

into her palm   then turned and

left the room

Drawing in Charcoal

The garden of the world has no limits,

except in your mind ~ Rumi

Sitting

propped up in bed

I look at the charcoal drawing

The one I sketched of the exotic model

I view the muscular torso

the outstretched legs

her arms draped over the chair

It isn't hers   of course

that body

This sinewy shape is mine

each tissue drawn taut

not willowy and at rest as she sat

but posed to push off at any moment

She slept as we drew

The electric heater keeping her warm

as our easels surrounded her throne

Bach played on

as our hands blackened with their work

After Seeing "Waiting on the Moon"

When the soul lies down in that grass the world

is too full to talk about ~ Rumi

Geraldine Stein had an angel

for a friend

Something we all wish we had

but hers was flesh and blood

A genius and an angel

What better combination could be found

than an angel who would say "yes"

and a writer

waiting peacefully

for the moon

to rise

over the trees

Breakfast at McDonald's

Where there is ruin, there is hope for a treasure ~ Rumi

The Lamia woman sits

holding her teeth in her scaly hand

The diluted tissue of her face

haughty above the Canadian Bacon

Her now read newspaper folds crisp

as she smacks her lips

The tip of her tongue darting out

to capture the bread crumb

at the corner of her wrinkled mouth

like a reptile at feeding

This distorted scene from the ancients

twists my vision

above my steaming coffee cup

as the aged woman restores her gleaming porcelain

and rises like a goddess

from the booth

A youth

in cotton Pacifics

brushes against her green and brown patterned pants

and she slides slippery

towards the dumpster with her bag

My eyes follow every movement

as she fills the depths

glancing over her shoulder

at the young Lycius

with the tennis racket

in white shorts

and sweatband

with that dulled twinkle in her eye

Snow Bombs

Anything you lose comes round in another form

~ Rumi

Have you ever noticed

how nature sometimes

tries to get you?

Like after a heavy spring snowstorm

and the trees are laden and

you're trying to have

a peaceful walk in the woods

and the trees drop their bombs

and you know they

were meant to scare

yet   you stay

But down deep you

feel that someone up there has

it in for you

Have you ever noticed that?

March Gravesite Visit

When one's sense perceives the hidden, the invisible

world becomes apparent to the whole

>   ~ Rumi

I recall that autumn day

we met at the graveside

They   in their black suits

I   feeling the chill of their greetings

You lie now beside your mother

who at eighty-three travelled the seas

carrying her own luggage

unwilling to concede

I remember your mauled hand

fingerless

consumed

by the combine

that harvest day

You   spending your youth

and manhood in solitude

Unable to extend that hand freely

until the last year of your life

When I picture you now it's in that straw hat

the one with the wide red band

setting smartly on your gray head

your silver Cadillac pulling into our drive

That last time

you came to say your goodbyes

to the home where I no longer lived

I said I would come

but   I couldn't

Yet   I remember

as I sit here among the marble headstones

feeling the cool spring breeze at my back

Ghazal of the Now

I want to sing like the birds sing, not worrying

about who hears or what they think ~ Rumi

I see the swagger of smoke

as numbed eyes invade mine

I see the conference room door open

and its obese women in black with gold necklace rise

If I could only see the brown man's face

with his vision intact fly

I see spirits of dust obliterate the tiles

as I smell the under-lust of droning breath

I want to feel the melodious rhythm

that pollutes the paneling   caresses the acoustical ceiling

Ah   don't let the risings of a monkish life

bury me within the cloistered weavings

Leave the philodendron to shelter the crayons

and the chalk lady to draw the door

The Crossroads

These pains you feel are messengers. Listen to them

~ Rumi

Funny   I never thought about it before

Iowa has only two highways

and

they meet right there

Yeah   that's the crossroads

right in the middle of the cornfield

Yeah   I never thought about it either

It's like the boy at the wrestling meet

when his arm snapped

the bone pushing out through his flesh

One woman screamed and ran out of the gym

It's kind of like that

Isn't it?

Well   maybe it's more like the Raccoon River

as it surges through the state

Remember last summer when it overflowed its banks?

Remember how everyone got nervous

How the basements flooded

How some people lost everything

because they had built on the flood plain?

Maybe it's more like that

Or maybe it's like that hailstorm

that hit down south

Remember how the hail was the size of a baseball

how it ruined the roofs

and your mom's siding had holes in it and

the tomato plants were beat to the ground?

Maybe it's more like that

Yeah   maybe

Maybe that's the crossroads

how we survive

Maneuvering the Big Dipper

We come spinning out of nothingness, scattering stars

like dust ~ Rumi

Last night I dreamed

I was dangling

from the Big Dipper

Once more I pushed

and swayed so smoothly

forward

I felt the warmth

as I let go

of the star behind

caught my breath

viewed the distance

of the next swing

calculated carefully

closed my eyes

and stretched out

my body

again

The Green Theatre

Look at love...how it tangles

with the one fallen in love ~ Rumi

With my sandals resting on the painted bench

I remember an earlier time when we sat here

The day I slipped up quietly behind you

embarrassed

You had your shirt off

basking in the hot summer sun

I had no desire   or did I

to see your naked flesh?

What did I want?

Snapping the twig

to announce my presence

knowing that you would understand

and cover yourself

Is this the same bench we sat on that day

discussing your art?

The rows are so deceiving in their sameness

It seems it is

for then   too

my legs dangled   My feet

unable to touch the ground

What are the two lovers doing in our green theatre?

Embracing as one

swaying to their music on the shaded stage

unaware that someone watches

as arm in arm they turn

and walk through the woods

choosing their path in unison

a chance we had

but never took

I turn and watch the four walking

The mother holds the hand of the youngest child

a boy in the red sweatshirt near her elbow

the father   fifteen yards ahead

Soon the boy runs to his father's side

and matches his gait

while the mother and daughter walk behind

only steps from our green theatre

That Night

Dancing is not just getting up painlessly,

like a leaf blown on the wind;

dancing is when you tear your heart out

and rise out of your body to hang

suspended between the worlds ~ Rumi

Rain was not far away

as we strolled Court Avenue

that night

when Baryshnikov

danced

You   dressed in black and white

your hair swept behind your earlobe

the dancers performing an arabesque in "Don Quixote"

I   sitting

mesmerized by the movements

At intermission we walked the carpeted halls

familiar eyes upon us

speaking of Gray's quest for a perfect moment

in "Swimming to Cambodian"

of Marilyn's part

as we settled ourselves for "Apollo"

You spoke of vapors

that surged through your veins

as I watched the dancers

and their radiance

lifted me

then

slowly

brought me back

again

Mikhail

Standing now

you motioned to the stage with your hands clasped

tossing your head like a pinto

Mikhail

That night

at the ballet

as the rain

slowly fell

on the refurbished umbrella

that leans lazily

by the cooling reflection pool

But once that pool   too

could not avoid death

as it inhaled the three-year-old child

into its slippery larynx

like a deep drag on a cigarette

Holding her lovingly

as if her years of dance

were a pagan god's sacrifice

Yet   she one day   too

will plie` again

perhaps upon Riga's soil

Oh   Mikhail

Mikhail

The Fish Hook

Mysteries are not to be solved: The eye goes blind

when it only wants to see why ~ Rumi

The pond is in pandemonium today

Searing robins shriek with the unexpected clime

The water spits at their sweeping dives

while massive snow bombs careen from the trees

like some mythic pie fight

It wasn't long ago

that it was summer at this arena

and I was searching for the fish hook

swaying from the sheltering sycamore

Do you see it? he asked

No

There   There it is   Look closely, he whispered

And there it was

just as he knew

So exquisite

dangling from the transparent line

So tiny

I don't know how he first saw it

Yet   he did

And he waited patiently

until I saw it too

That day we watched the young girl on the hill

crying while her mate waited

She squalled so lustily

in her descent

The tears subsiding only when

the goal was near

I   watching solemnly

as the fish hook netted the breeze

The Park Pond

Who could be so lucky? Who comes to a lake for water

and sees the reflection of moon ~ Rumi

How can stagnant water have such fascination?

We strangers sit on the bench

and gaze

into the depths

Each with our own thoughts

Like the ancient basket weavers

who squatted in the Arizona cliff dwellings

The Universe breathes in

then out

like a dancer

in a Hopi pipe ritual

spreading spiritual energy

into the wild

desert of Pueblo Bonito

much like the glow of

this muddy water before us

Blinking Neon

Not only the thirsty seek the water,

the water as well seeks the thirsty ~ Rumi

You stood

under the park shelter

as rain

simmered down

Your legs spread wide

like Tom Buchanan

before his glorious house

Your taut back

in shadows

We watched

two white-tailed deer

feeding in the distance

before your solemn voice

split the silence

with your denial

while lightening bugs

blinked neon

and I thought of the unattainable

green light

at the end of the pier

The Intrusion

The truth was a mirror in the hands of God.

It fell, and broke into pieces. Everybody took a

piece of it, and they looked at it and thought

they had the truth ~ Rumi

Tramping the path

we felt mud suck our toes

as you spoke

of a fifteen-year-old girl who

gave her virginity as a present

in a hayloft

I   laughing

while you

growled your masculinity

I recalled that other day at the baseball field

when I had grinned nervously

so long ago

thinking there had been a home run

only to discover

the game was forgotten

You   expressing your ambition

I   hesitating as mud leached through my toes

Moving forward   our paths divided

as we talked of friendship

Your belief that a man and a woman could never develop

the bond that two men are capable of

Hiding my disappointment

I tugged to be free

as you spoke of your career as an artist

and I picked up a twisted stick to clean off my sole

realizing how the twilight before you

was that same interrupted dream

I had had as a child

before I was forced to sleep

You hunched your shoulders

and walked away

leaving me

standing

silently

working at my task

A Sunday After

The cure for pain is in the pain ~ Rumi

The world looks less menacing from here

after my climb up the steep grass-covered hill

The pond's water isn't as muddy

from this higher vantage point

A young man

strokes the curls of his lover on the blanket

as blue bicycles roll down the path

while a cluster of teens

descend slowly

chatting   laughing   steps light

A woman in tan shorts

balances a seashell

in her palm and I know

the swollen bruises

of my wounds have begun to fade

Clinging Snow

Shine like the whole universe is yours ~ Rumi

The branches are bare

Heavy snow clings to the northern bark

like periwinkles sucking chilled boulders of the

ocean's crevices

Soon the snow   too   will slip to the ground

I watch the Noah's Ark truck

leaving the park

and recall those days

when I too clung

unable to let go

Women run by in gray jogging suits

hoods up   protected from the cold

running their ten miles a day

Aberrations of melodies

Alert to their progress

I sit alone

knowing that I too have been running

since I dropped to the ground

Sacred Anasazi World

And still, after all this time, the Sun has never said to the Earth, "You owe me." ~ Rumi

Sometimes I remember

and wonder

what it all meant

the nomadic movement of the bike wheels

the talks of the classics

the moments of unspoken feelings

Nothing?

I wonder

as I balance my checkbook

and reconstruct

the eight-hundred piece jigsaw puzzle

of the female figure

Much like the task of Wetherill who

devoted his life to the ruins

of the sacred Anasazi world

and was shot from his horse

on that quiet early morning

in Mesa Verde   so long ago

The Riderless Horse

You must ask for what you really want ~ Rumi

Lying in the hotel bed

with a flowered bedspread crumpled at my feet

I smile at the green and tan picture

of the horse without a rider

that hangs nearby

My daughter showers

as the Chipmunks sing their strange melodies

on the Saturday morning cartoons

This morning

of the first trip

we take away from my new home

Forever in another state now

I stretch luxuriously

with my knowledge

The Third Tier

Flow down and down in always widening rings of being

~ Rumi

He said the phrase with humor

as I slid by

taking my seat behind

Going down to the third tier? he asked

I smiled

thinking about our last meeting

when she joined us

How she drummed the table

glancing at the time

We speaking about beliefs

or lack of

Her dark glasses hiding her eyes

hands exposed

She   having bought strawberries

to place gingerly in each glass

and

after

cheesecake

We   leaning close   talking

across the warmed oak table

until the clock struck the appointed hour

In Maria's Waking Dream

Whoever finds love beneath hurt and grief

disappears into emptiness

with a thousand new disguises ~ Rumi

Sprigs of persimmon sprout through cracks

Tendrils caress bare legs

Maria lies still as a southern chameleon

resting in the twilight near a public sidewalk

watching a lady dancer who fills her vision

fade in and out with awkward maneuvers

as if blown by a harmonious torrential gale

the solid blackness of the dramatic backdrop

causing the mirage's chalky gown to glow

A centipede creeps

across Maria's exposed ankle

and she shivers

while a shrouded performer balances

on an elevated seawall

arms raised   delicate fingers spread

gown billowing

beckoning to the woman below

Wide-eyed   Maria reaches down to

rub her thigh

groans

then turns her head

on her pillow

once again

The Disappearing String

The same wind that uproots trees makes the grass shine

~ Rumi

I dreamed the balloons tied to my house

draped over the chipped paint

bringing beauty to the exterior

I watched as the man walked several paces

his belly pushing out from his trousers

a cap matching their chalkiness

His fingers loosened

and molecules of color

drifted high like a kite's slippery tail

to float over the river

mixing with the heavens

descending

on someone else's house

Days Gone By

Thankfulness brings you to the place where

the Beloved lives ~ Rumi

Misty sands

with hooked-nosed man

of smiling eyes

brings memories

of aiming arms

Horned beasts watch

near the flaming fire

one lone figure

lying

on her straw pallet

as brownish red centipedes

slink down her legs

A boy plays mumble-d-peg

while early celebrants hold each other

in abeyance

near amused citizens

who sharpen their quills

to capture the scene

A storyteller

sits on a rotten stump

and begins her tale

like the opium drugged

mariner who held the

wedding guests attention

near the open doorway

in days gone by

Mount Ayr

Let the beauty of what you love be what you do ~ Rumi

Can you imagine being from such a place?

Nestled nowhere

Remote from others

Raised among tractors that endlessly

furrow the rows

To wake up each morning

yawning exquisitely

To look out your window

at the twisted solitary elm

and beyond to perceive the subterranean soil

stretching far to the heavens

envisioning the mirage at the horizon

Knowing the bountiful black earth breathes

here on your piece of land in Mount Ayr

Laying Sod

Set your life on fire. Seek those who fan your flames

~ Rumi

Today they laid the sod

that stood in clumps of stacked profusion

ready to cover the prepared earth

Stopping for a moment

we watched the men's progress

slow

meticulous

forming cut patterns

within the greened grass

beside the backdrop

of dark scrubs

Like the bush that you

in your cowboy hat

pulled the sprigs from to

make your point about the here

and now as I smiled

and viewed other workers

over your shoulder

laboring   mysteriously at their greening task

Blow it Up

The soul is here for its own joy ~ Rumi

Two ink spots

in the distance

transverse the space

as the wayfarer

sits silent

in consternation

and finely-veined hands

droop in hypnotic

alpha-state awareness

The poet

a boat captain

gone mad

as she

daydreams into the night of stars

White Wolf at Her Side

My soul is from elsewhere, I'm sure of that, and I intend to end up there ~ Rumi

I see her

at Glacier Bay

An opaque figure

with serene expression

and folded hands

Whirling snow

encircles her skirt

as a white wolf

at her side

leads her forward

into a crevice

of crystal vapor

while angelic snowflakes

lace her hair

Balloon Days

What strikes the oyster shell does not damage the pearl

~ Rumi

God's name isn't damnit

now what kind of thing is that

to put on a cap

worn by a farmer

who smiles

enjoying his joke

as you read it

in the A&W restaurant

while fries sizzle in their basket

and August brushed skies

sweep the horizon in

red

ochre

    blue

                and silver

as heavy wicker baskets

slowly descend

swept in gold

underlaid in oozing browns

There Is More Light

When you feel a peaceful joy, that's when you

are near truth ~ Rumi

I look around the room

the girl in the ponytail

and dark blue sweater

raises her chin

eyes sparkling

A key

lost?

Found?

Where?

Somewhere else?

She seems to think

not as she writes furiously

trying to capture

that quiet light within

Pelican Totem

Respond to every call that excites your spirit ~ Rumi

Buoyant   unselfish

battling trauma

almost driven to extinction by DDT

but saved by the notch of time

Impassioned to soar   climb   plunge-dive

                                        to choose

                                        to love

She ascends

wings touching the Divine

then plummets toward the water

                                        shattering the surface

Blessed with Choice

Most people guard against the fire and thus end up in it

~ Rumi

The door is open

The view a luminous

sapphire   crimson   and silver vista

of rippling waters

soaring birds

haunted dark-leafed mangrove

and hurricane-twisted sand

She stands

gripping the frame

enduring the flames of indecision

not ready to open her eyes

and step through

Ole House

All despair is followed by hope; all darkness is followed

by sunshine ~ Rumi

The woman in the straw hat hums

as she seasons and pan-fries

the afternoon catch

Her faded fishing rod

leans against a plastic bucket

while her cat's tail weaves

then taps the wooden floor

Her questioning eyes

dart to the paned window

toward the echo of the sea

click of halyard against mast

But   within this ole house

she remains

inspired and comforted

by the salt-weathered clapboards

The Pelican

You were born with wings, why prefer to crawl

through life? ~ Rumi

Head poised   she hovers

aged wings spread wide

before landing

in the protected mangrove

as dark waters lap beneath

Say Yes

Be like melting snow, wash yourself of yourself ~ Rumi

Dressed in a brown gauze gown

with a brass snake encircling her torso

the woman sat yoga-style on a bed of snow

speaking of the seven Hindu chakras

Whorls of energy

emanating from force centers

Listening   I closed my eyes

and the snake enlivened

tightening its grip

around her vulnerable neck

until the serpent's mouth widened

and transformed

into a lotus blossom

as the snow beneath us

thawed and flowed into the nearby river

Acknowledgments

I thank the following people for their editorial advice, feedback and encouraging support throughout this project: Marjorie Carlson Davis, Claudia Bischoff, Suzanne Kelsey, Ellen Larson, Marsha Perlman and Jeannette Batko. I also extend my gratitude to the professors who served on my dissertation committee for my Doctor of Arts degree at Drake University. Many of these poems were critiqued and accepted by them: Thomas Swiss, Max Autrey, David Foster, Kenneth Miller, and my first reader, Ruth Doty. As several individual pieces are published in literary journals, I thank those editors for their support.

A special thank you goes to fine artists Peg Cullen and Andi McCarter who created the works of art that grace the cover. Another goes to Lorraine Walker Williams of ARTPoems 2013 for including me in this collaborative production where Dance Alliance dancer Lydia Frantz transformed "Say Yes" into interpretative expression. To photographers Lynn Berreitter and Jan Palmer, and all the other visual artists who provided inspiration, I tip my cap.

To my children, Conrad and Danielle and my life partner, Tom, the words 'thank you' are not enough.

And finally, to my mother, the woman who always encouraged me to write and read—I'm sure she's above the clouds fishing and continuing to write her own poems. Thanks, Mom.

About the Poet and Author

Joyce (j.d.) Daniels` prize-winning prose and poetry has appeared in various publications, including: *The Broad River Review, The Sylvan Echo, The Elkhorn Review, riverbabble* and *Doorknobs & BodyPaint Fantastic Flash Fiction: An Anthology.* "Nancy's Woodcut" won second place in a contest sponsored by Emerson College/Cambridge University in England. She is listed in the Iowa Arts Council and Poets & Writers` Directories, and is an active member of PEN Women of Southwest Florida.

The Old Wolf Lady: A Biography was published by a grant from The Iowa Arts Council. Being a co-founder and an editor of *Prairie Wolf Press Review* helps her keep her fingers on the pulse of contemporary literature.

Besides her passion for writing, she enjoys travel, kayaking, walking and laughing with her friends and family. Her social networks include: Facebook, Linkedin, She Writes and Twitter.

Her Website: www.authorsden.com/joyceadaniels

www.ingramcontent.com/pod-product-compliance
Lightning Source LLC
Chambersburg PA
CBHW031453040426
42444CB00007B/1079